SPOKEN WORDS

© J.K. Cloinger 2014

ISBN 978-1-312-28109-7

A CAT

By the door a cat rested
watching a ball of yarn
slowly gets up and
goes to the barn

there a mouse upon a rail
caught a watchful eye
darted past an out stretched paw
and gave a joyful sigh

bored of tiring games
the cat fell asleep
but kept a watchful eye
for things that creep

awaken by an unknown sound
he runs into the house
there he finds his food
better than a mouse

a bowl of milk he drinks
washes his face
he scurries back to
his favorite hiding place

just a lazy cat
never in a rush
now fast asleep
so be quiet, Hush!

A Child's Dreams

A basket full of dreams carried by a child
can tame the wildest beast
and turn a flower wild

Can make a sunset pale,
out shine the brightest star
make the wisest man
seek knowledge from afar

Take a broken heart mend
it with just a smile
make a single step seem like a mile
turn a darken night into a sunny day

Make all the heartaches up and fly away
make the whole world tremble
with undying love
For a child's dreams are sent from God above

A DOLL'S MEMORY

Over in the corner upon a dusty shelf
sits an old ragged doll all by herself
her hair is faded,
her dress torn and gray
her shoes are gone now,
she was a beauty
in her day

She once had raven hair,
skin smooth and clear
a dress of purple velvet,
eyes without a tear
as years pass her by
she grows old with grace
for she knows within her heart,
she will never be replaced

She sits alone upon her shelf,
silent as can be
this is where she belongs
in the dreams of memories
her little girl is grown now,
with children of her own
but she still remembers all
the love she has ever known

A FANTASY WORLD

A fantasy life is near at hand
some will never understand
close my eyes, dreams my dreams
plot my destruction, scheme my schemes
slowly now I drift away
going back to yesterday
caring not who I am
don't really give a damn
pills rule my life
fill my head with strife
take me up, bring me down
twist my mind, throw me round
where am I today
how can I really say
come tomorrow I'll be here
that is truly my only fear

Now I've gone to sleep
my life I do not keep
can I live, will I die?
don't know, I'm too high
like a cloud I drift by
full of hate and will not try
help me, soon I'll be dead
now I lay down to rest my head
pop my pills, receive my dreams
plot my death, scheme my scheme
I lie in peace now at last
my fantasy world has finally past.

A Gift Of Friendship

Through
their laughter
their generous support
their honesty
their companionship
I find comfort and meaning in my life.

Through
their smiles
their tears
their pain
their devotion
I find understanding and
compassion in my life.

Through
their determination
their forgiveness
their kindness
their silence
I find inspiration and serenity in my life.

Through
their hopes
their faith
their presence
their patience
I find love and happiness in my life.

A MAN-A BOY

Underneath a tree he sat
Looking all alone and yet
Upon his face was a look
Only seen in a picture book

His eyes were like a fountain deep
Into which the stars did creep
His hair, a flowing mass of yellow
He was a handsome sort of fellow

He was serene upon his throne
Though he seemed so all alone
His world was full of glee
At least it seemed to be

A man of the world
With a curious curl
Just a boy of three
Who belongs to me.

A MEMORY

Last night a memory
came to visit me
it flew through my heart
and sat itself free

It gave me a kiss
upon my tender cheek
and flew through the house
playing hide-n-seek

It flew up the stairs
down through the hall
then it came back
and stood by the wall

It looked at me
and began to cry
it said my name
and told me why

I love you dearly
we're never apart
and with those words
it flew back into my heart.

A REMEMBRANCE

Once upon a dewy morn
a small sweet rose was born
the trees were budding in the lane
as I sat beside the window pane

A field of wildflowers grow nearby
as a young bird learns to fly
a butterfly landed near the wall
where the leafs land in Fall

Wildflowers, birds, and butterflies
dewy morns and soft heard cries
a memory true to my heart
is where a remembrance has to start

A Silent Thought

A little girl sat silently
beneath a tree of green
she marveled the mystery
of all the wondrous things

she watched the gentle grass
as it blew to and fro
she saw a golden butterfly
put on a joyous show

she saw the raindrops
as they came slowly down
upon the flowers it did fall
to spread a melodic sound

she watched as the sun
faded behind the hill
in a silent thought
she knew the world was still

A SMILE-A FROWN

A SMILE UPON HER FACE
TO REPLACE
A SADDEN HEART
ONLY PART
OF LIFE ALONE
HURT UNKNOWN
TEARS TO CRY
ALL A LIE
NOT THE END
TRY AGAIN
UPSIDE DOWN
NOW A FROWN
GOES HER WAY
DAY BY DAY
ALL THE DOUBT
GONE WITHOUT
A TRACE OF PAIN
TO LOVE AGAIN.

A TOKEN

I looked up in the sky one day,
 after the rain was through
I saw a multi-colored rainbow,
 peeking out of the blue
I never knew why or how,
 that rainbow came to be
Till one day someone I know,
told this story to me
Forty days and nights it rained,
 earth and man gone, not a trace
Only one named Noah,
 was spared by God's grace
A mighty Ark he did build, and filled it two by two
Of every living creature there, as God told him to do
After the waters were gone away
and the Ark came to rest
The Lord made a promise that he would do his best
To never again destroy everything
 that once was made
Just to rid the world of sin,
 for it was the earth that paid
The rainbow is God's token between
 himself and the earth
And Noah is the father of all the new rebirth
The rainbow is a reminder of the
 covenant God will keep
For every living creature be they awake or asleep
So look at that rainbow close,
remember how it came to be
A promise of God's heavenly
love he gives to you and me .

AGES OF MEMORIES

Sitting by the fireplace
her heart all aglow
as she slowly turns the pages
of the memories she knows

there she is at one
in a dress of satin red
with pretty little bonnet
tied upon her dainty head

here she is at ten
with dollie and her dad
her mother was so happy
times were never sad

here again at twenty
and never been kissed
she's holding out for love
not caring what she missed

there she is at forty
a husband and three kids
loving each one special
for the many things they did

now alone at eighty
her life is almost done
are there any regrets?
no, she has not a one

closing up the album
of memories she keeps
she gently drifts away
into a never-ending sleep

Becoming Whole

Me, myself and I
decided to have a talk
so we all took off
for a long, long walk

I could not forgive myself
for things that were said
it just wasn't me alone
but all of us instead

Neither I nor myself
would repeat the words
so it was me alone
that forgot what was heard

I became upset with myself
and then began to cry
I couldn't understand
myself or me or why

Without myself and me
I am not alive
for it takes all of us
in order to survive.

IF YOU BELIEVE

The hobbits are funny creatures
they have the strangest features
some are fat and some are tall
some are short and some are small.

The elves live in trees, forests deep
they're always busy, never sleep
they are magic, did you know
but they never let it show.

The unicorns are not elves or trolls
they have the purest hearts and souls
they always help, they never hinder
they are so kind, they speak so tender.

If you see a dragon someday soon
just say hello and sign a tune
he will dance and play with you
and you will feel the magic, too.

Unicorns, dragons, hobbits and elves
are here inside of our very selves
wish hard enough, you will see
fairytales are meant to be.

To unlock the door, no complications
just use your own imagination
it's the key to untold riches
it makes the world fulfill your wishes.

Between the Soldier and the Man

They sat there talking to each other
one was someone's son,
the other someone's brother
one was dressed in uniform
with Private on his sleeve
he was headed home now
on temporary leave

One was going to see his mother,
he'd been away awhile
he couldn't wait to see her,
just a few more miles
one's name was Danny,
the others name was Dan
one was a soldier,
the other just a man

One fights for freedom
so others can live
one lives for justice with
all he can give
they talked on for hours
of things they never knew
love, honor and country
just to name a few

At the end of their conversation
they each would understand
there could be no secrets between
the soldier and the man.

Can.......

A gentle touch, a warm embrace
make the deepest soul confess?
A tender kiss, a loving word
make the unspoken heart be heard?
A caring smile, a fond embrace
bring a tear of joy to your face?
A breaking heart, a doubting mind
make a true love hard to find?

THE CATERPILLAR

The caterpillar has legs a-plenty
Whereas the earthworm hasn't any

The caterpillar is covered with hair
Whereas the snake is very bare

The caterpillar becomes a butterfly
Whereas crickets just jump high

The caterpillar eats leafs and plants
Whereas the aardvark eats only ants

The caterpillar is strange indeed
Whereas grass is only seed

The caterpillar never talks
He just walks and walks and walks

CHILDHOOD DREAMS

The sweat pours from under his hat
as he ever so slowly steps up to bat
he looks out across all the bases
staring into all the waiting faces
elbows bent, back is straight
he swings, misses, kicks the plate
takes his stand and tries again
if he misses they can't win

Slowly grips the bat with both hands
watches the ball to see where it lands
strike two is called, can this be
only one more turn, then strike three
once more he steps up to bat
turns around his baseball hat
hits the ball with mighty force
sends it sailing, off coarse

Two strikes, now a foul
he hears the crowd as they howl
bat in hand and now he swings
hits the ball into the wings
across the field he sends it soaring
fans stand up and they are roaring
he runs the bases one by one
no one can stop him till he's done

Across the plate he flies
safe is what the umpire cries
then he wakes up the dream is done
once more comes the morning sun
just an old man pushing a broom
long ago forgotten in a dusty old room
dreams of childhood linger here
keeping an old man alive year after year

Clouds

Clouds are the strangest things
They float across the sky,
Do you know how they got that way?
Well, neither do I.

They make the weirdest shapes
As they float to and fro,
How they hang there
I will never really know.

They're fluffy like marshmallows
All billowy and white,
Some are dark and ominous
On a stormy night.

They serve whatever purpose
They were meant to do
And are the home
For little angles, too.

Every time I see one
On a cloudy day,
I wonder in awe
As it floats away.

COLORS

The colors of the American flag
have been shot at, stomped on,
burnt and dragged
have flown high on battlefields
on home and foreign land
have been placed with respect
and honor in loved ones hands

have stood for freedom,
peace and glory
have told each generation,
America's story
have hung in awesome beauty
for hundreds of years
have felt rain, snow, heat,
wind and tears

have waved proudly, no matter
where or how long
have had words written
about them in song
have been made into shoes,
hats and shirts
have known plenty of love
and unspeakable hurts

have been saluted, praised and cursed
have always been called on first
have never faltered, will always wave
over the land of the free and
the home of the brave

DARKNESS

Beneath the covers
I did crawl
To escape
The shadowed wall

Things of the night
Come at dark
Cat's meow
Dogs bark

Light goes out
Imagination begins
In total darkness
No one wins

In my bed
Now I hide
With my teddy
By my side

Morning comes
I awake
Was it real
Or a glad mistake?

DOMESTIC GODDESS

I am a woman of the eighties
whose life is very modest
my career is very exciting
I am a domestic goddess

I cook, I sew, I clean all day
I vacuum and I mop
I am always doing something
never time to stop
my house is not a castle high
my husband's not a king
I have no crown or diamonds
just a simple golden ring

My dresses are not satin or lace
my car is not a coach
my life is quite complete
with a novel approach
I don't receive riches
for the services I render
the love and understanding
is always sweet and tender

Of all the jobs I could have
this one is the best
domestic goddess of my household
tops all the rest.

EVER SEEN?

Ever seen a dragon climb a cherry tree?
Ever seen a cow fly like a bee?
Ever seen an elephant drive a big blue truck?
Ever seen a horse quack like a duck?

Ever seen a dog with a bunny nose?
Ever seen a snake turn into a garden hose?
Ever seen a frog live in a shoe?
Ever seen a giraffe that was crystal blue?

Just silly questions ask of me each day
From a six year old with a lot to say
A lot of silly things that could very well be
But, not in my lifetime will I come to see

Eyes Of A Poet

Through a poet's eyes we see
The things that life can give
A tree, a flower, a bird that sings
A chance to be forever free

Through the verse of poetry
We travel far and wide
To distant lands and mountains
To heart and heavens high

We see the world through their eyes
As only they can tell
The poet's world is full of joy
And makes our hearts swell.

Family Photos

it's that time of year
for family photos to be shot
but as usual
they all seem to have forgot
mama in her curlers
brother has no socks
dad didn't shave and
granny's in a smock

Now we have to hurry
to get ourselves prepared
now where is that camera
as if I really cared
the camera is ready
the time is so right
the ways things are going
we'll be here all night

Grandpa lost his glasses
Juniors lost his shoe
sister has the sneezes
and me, I have the flu
next year will be better
I really hope it will
or we may be here forever
trying to get a picture still

Family photos can be nice
they can be rather fun
but if your family is like mine
you may never, ever get one

FLOWER OR SEED

In the garden of life
you're meant to be a flower
you bud and blossom
every waking hour

you stretch and grow
nurtured by the rain
you drink your fill of love
and go to sleep again

if someone cares for you
you grow up big and strong
you are safe from everything
you can do no wrong

without the love and caring
you become a lonely weed
you are picked from the garden
and returned to the seed

GOD'S YARD SALE

If God had a yard sale
Oh, the rare things we might find
Like hope, faith and charity
Or maybe our peace of mind
Little boxes full of shining moments
Mixed in with rainbows bright
Could we maybe somehow find?
That true and guiding light

Would there be bouquets of flowers?
All lined up in tiny vases
Which, when given honestly
Would put smiles on lonely faces
Perhaps we find love and forgiveness
Wrapped up in pretty colored bows
So we could take them home
To the loved ones whom we know

Would there be a special something?
We could get to heal all our sins
So they could be washed away
To start our lives again
Maybe a little table
Where dreams and prayers are sold
Something to help us through
All the heartaches we hold
For those rare and precious things
What would the prices be?
At God's heavenly yard sale
Everything he has to offer us is free

Going, Going, Gone

The last days of summer are nearing
I hate to watch them as they go
Now I must start to really think
About the ice, wind and the snow

Somewhere in between, fall will arrive
And leaves I again will rake
So goodbye my sweet friend summer
I just can't catch a break

No more lemonade by the poolside
Only shades of fall and colder days
Why can't summer last all year long?
Why does it have to leave me in a haze?

So farewell dear friend, ta, ta, goodbye
Your warmness I will surely endear
Oh, wait a minute, I forgot
You'll be back again next year.

HANNA

Her name was Hanna, she lived all alone
her husband was departed her children gone
she had a one-eyed dog and three legged cat
a cow named Bessie who wore a blue hat
she sang in the choir with old man Brown
he was a preacher from way cross town
after church dinners ,they always talked
when it turned dusk, they often walked
down by the river where wild flowers grow
what they did there ,no one knows
Hanna was ninety, the preacher eighty
he was a gentleman ,but she was no lady
when they returned clothes all askew
people in the town were sure they knew
Hanna's hat was off, her dress awry
the preacher's jacket, not very dry
her hair had fallen all out of place
both were blushing ,red in the face
the preacher said thank you, went on his way
see you next Sunday was all Hanna could say
so do you know what went on in the woods
did Hanna ask the preacher to deliver the goods
did they have a thing for each other
was old lady Hanna the preacher's lover
people will whisper and many will talk
none will ever know the reason for that walk
Hanna's in her house without any temptations
for preacher Brown showed
her the way to salvation

Harrison The Dragon

Harrison was a dragon
who lived in mountains high
he was a brave and fearless tot
who tried to learn to fly

He use to watch his father
as he flew across the land
and hoped that someday soon
he would be just as grand

His mother told him, soon my son
as you begin to grow
you will learn the secrets
that all brave dragons know

Then one day it happened
as his mother said it would
he flew across the valley
where the big tall mountains stood

The secrets of the dragons' flight
can never be revealed
for if it were known to all
the dragons fate would be sealed

HENRIETTA

Henrietta was a classy hen
who sat upon her perch
she never ran, she never squawked
she was always on the search

now rooster Dan knew her well
and he began to crow
but Henrietta didn't care
she thought he was to slow

she walked the barnyard over
looking for a mate
she never thought of Dan
until it was too late

when she went looking
for mighty rooster Dan
she couldn't find him anywhere
for he was roasting in a pan

so she gathered up his feathers
upon them she did lay
and there she did remain
till her dying day

ILLUSIONS OF SUMMER

Ice cream cones melting fast
The loveliest of days never last
Wild under the burning sun
Jumping in puddles just for fun

Carriage rides in the park
Stolen kisses after dark
Recycled promises we can't keep
Erased emotions than ran so deep

These illusions come one by one
Summer is over now and done
Scrapbook clippings in a book
There for all to take a look.

Imprisoned By Silence

I have been here before
Motionless and depressed,
Pain surging through me
Remembering endless tears,
In silent nightmares
Someone touches me,
Overcome with fear
Needing always to
Escape from it all
Danger lurks near.

Beneath me the blood flows
Yet I feel nothing.

Shhhh, listen
 I hear someone coming,
 Lying here I cry
Eyes looking,
Nothing there
Clearly I can
Endure no more.

IS

A pocket full of poetry
Is a basket full of dreams
A broken heart upon the ground
Is busted at the seams

A river full of teardrops
Is a life full of woe
A long road to walk
Is which way do I go

A simple little question
Is a difficult answer
A man who is a singer
Is not really a dancer

A person who laughs
Is one who also cries
A world who lives
Is one that surely dies

A life full of heartaches
Is a bitter one to live
A heart that is loving
Is one that will always give

JOURNEY OF A MEMORY

Through the rivers of my mind
memories float a new
some are very special, some sad, a few
they turn the winding curves,
of long forgotten ways
and end up in the meadows
of lost and lonely days

From the wondering meadow,
through the forest deep
they cross the bridge of
our restless sleep
across the skies of yesterdays,
they slowly turn about
gently through the heart they
find their way out

They linger in the valley of
long lost dreams
and sometimes drown in
a bitter stream
from a river of remembrance,
across the span of years
we always have a reason to
let a memory near
the journey of a memory is a
long and lonely one
a special recollection
and then it is gone.

JUST YOU

Who is that lady standing over there?
the one with the tears in her eyes
she seems so gentle and caring to me
who could have made her cry?

Looking in her face covered with age
the years have been many and long
she seems so lost now, standing there
singing the same old song

Her gray hair is tinted with silver
those brown eyes have grown pale
her hands are wrinkled with time now
her burdens she wears like a veil

Standing in front of the mirror
reflections always shine through
what seems like someone else
turns out to be just you.

LITTLE GIRL LOST

Over in the corner, she sits all alone
waiting for someone to take her home
she doesn't remember where she was yesterday
she remembers the pain, but not the way.

She's only fourteen and a woman full grown
trying to fight for a life of her own
she's tired and she feels so sad
she dreams of the good life she never had

Hopes and dreams shattered on the floor
a hard awakening with the slamming door
no one cares how she looks or how she feels
she looks in her pocket for a handful of pills

Sitting alone, no one seems to see her strife
a little girl lost in a fantasy world
liquor and pills keep her forever there
until her mind is gone, she doesn't care

She cries for help, but no one will come
only her pills can keep her lost and numb
she slowly falls upon the ground and cries
and that is where she sadly stays and dies.

Long Ago

Long ago the tangles of his golden hair
covered the emptiness of my open hand

Long ago the twinkle of his dark blue eyes
calmed the fears of my angry soul

Long ago the laughter from his tiny mouth
turned all the darkness to sunshine

Long ago the touch of his small hand
took all the doubts from within

Long ago he gave me hope, joy and understanding
and then like the wind he was gone

Love For A Pet

Upon the floor he lies
Not a care in sight
He may just stay there
Till the early morning light

He sometimes goes for a walk
Or cuddles in the chair
Sometimes in the bed
I gently stroke his hair

He chases all the birds
He digs holes in the dirt
He always comes to me
When he gets a little hurt

His hair is smoky white
His eyes are crystal blue
He does the funniest things
I've ever seen him do

At night he comes to me
And tells me of his day
He is my pet cat
And he has so much to say

I listen to his purr
And he licks my hand
A love for a pet isn't so hard
If you take time to understand

MAMA'S HEART

Mama's heart has been broken
by those she loves best
for they have gone and left her
they have flown the nest

She didn't want to let them go
she knew it would be hard
they will no longer be there
playing in the yard

She put away the baby things
no longer do they fit
she gave away the rocker
upon which they sit

Mama's heart hides many secrets
that may never be told
she keeps her children there
more precious than gold

Though mama's heart was broken
she does so understand
she has to break the ties
and still hold out her hand.

Mama's Dance

Went to a dance last Saturday night
looked across the room and
saw a terrible sight
there was mama dressed up to the nines
dancing with a man who
was older than time

They were twirling and
swirling round and round
when all of a sudden they both fell down
Mama's hat flew north,
her dress went south
everyone stopped and opened their mouth

The old man's shoe flew off and hit the wall
his pants came down, but that's not all
The music stopped,
the crowd gathered round
they both lay there,
together upon the ground
in disbelief I stared
and stood frozen by the door
Mama's voice rang out from across the floor
You silly old fool,
can't you take no for an answer
I told you I'm not a stripper, I'm a dancer.

Memories

I remember when I was three
little girl with long brown hair
a dolly and a purple dress
a dog, a cat, a rocking chair.

I remember when I was nine
I jumped rope, I ran a race
had strawberry popsicle
all over my little face.

I remember when I was twenty
a mother of a boy of two
trying the best I can
at what I need to do.

I remember when I was forty
a lifetime of pain and sorrow
trying to forget all the bad
praying for a better tomorrow.

I remember when I was sixty
three sons, that love me true
a better understanding of
the things I cannot do.

I remember all the years past
and the things that I see
are all that make up
this woman that is me.

Nothing to Wear

I'm in despair
I have nothing to wear,
If I were a bear
I could wear my hair.

People might stare
But I don't care,
I can go anywhere
That I dare.

I could go to the fair
With a white hare,
They might glare
At such a rare pair.

So please beware
Try not to stare,
I'm just bare
Cause I've nothing to wear.

Once In A

Beautiful, shimmering light
Lead me thru the darkest night
Unveil the world fast asleep
Engulf the ocean , oh so deep

Make your presence known to me
Open my eyes so I may see
Once in a lifetime you come along
Never ending mystery, then you're gone

PHOTOGRAPH

An old photograph
worn thin with age
I found hidden there
upon a forgotten page

The corners were torn
the colors almost faded
I tried to see
when it had been dated

The face seemed so familiar
although I could not remember
I think it was taken
sometime in September

Was it Christmas morning
or maybe a summer dance
maybe a sweetheart
that I met by chance

It's so hard to recall
when the memory goes
just like an old photo
that nobody knows

An old, old picture
lost in the years
covered with dust
till somebody cares

POETRY AND SUNSHINE

Poetry and sunshine
upon a rainy day
can soon chase
all the blues away

Sunshine to warm you
poetry to read
nurtured by love
grown from a seed

Poets

painters of the soul
are what poets are to me
they can paint a picture
of what poetry can be.

the colors that they use
are so bright and bold
listen to the tales of all
the stories they have told.

a poem is a masterpiece
created by a poet's heart
doesn't matter where it ends
or where it may start

QUESTIONS OF A CHILD

Why are zebras mild?
Why are tigers wild?
Why do birds fly so fast?
Why do rainbows never last?
Why are all clouds so white?
Why does day turn to night?
Why does the moon replace the sun?
Why I have freckles and you have none?
Such a lot of questions
As silly as can be
If you don't answer them
They'll ask till Eternity!!!!!!

QUESTIONS

DO I DARE?
DO I NOT?
IF I DON'T
SO WHAT?
WILL I SEE?
WILL I HEAR?
IF I DO
IS IT CLEAR?
DO I HAVE?
DO I GET?
ALL I WANT
NO, NOT YET
IS THIS STUPID?
I GUESS SO
I MAY BE CRAZY
I JUST DON'T KNOW
IT MAKES NO SENSE
IT ONLY RHYMES
IT MAY GET BETTER
WITH THE TIMES.

REFLECTIONS

As I stood before the mirror
Looking back to yesterday
The golden, brownish hair
Was replaced with silver grey

The blue eyes that were clear once
Now sadly show my life
Baby, toddler, teen
Woman, mother, wife

The wrinkles I cannot smooth
They age more with each year
They stare back at me
Among my doubting fears

The mirror tells no lies
The picture is true to me
It shows an older version
Of the youngster I should be

Is she who I am?
Or who I once was?
Can it truly matter?
What she really was

Before the mirror now
I wonder when she departed
That lovely little girl
From where my whole life started

SOLDIER

I am an American soldier, born in the land of the free
I was chosen to protect the freedom of you and me
I will do my best to stand tall, steadfast and bold
I have courage, pride and honor that I bravely uphold

I will face each enemy and put forth all that I can give
I will stand and sacrifice so that others may live
I carry in my heart what others will never see
I live with the memories of what a war can be

I watch each day as others around me slowly fall
I wait ready and willing to answer my call
I am a father, brother, husband. Soldier and son
I will stay here till the final battle is done

I do not have a chose in the things that I must do
I proudly stand up for the red, white and blue
I lay down at night and silently pray
I will wake tomorrow to see another day

I use my helmet as a pillow, my gun as a shield
I am one among thousands here on this battlefield
I dream of family and loved ones left behind
I keep them close to me in the corners of my mind

I face each day as best I can
I do what I must and try to understand
I will give my life, my heart and my soul to be
An American soldier back home in the land of the free.

SPIRIT

Alone at the head of the stairs
I sit with head in hand
trying now to somehow see
what I just cannot understand

Back and forth my memory races
shooting through my broken heart
tears are falling from my eyes
in my soul is where it starts

A spirit of days gone by
came to visit for awhile
to take away a sadden heart
and replace it with a smile

A gentle giving spirit
sat with me and told me much
then flew softly away
and left a tender touch

Squirrel's Adventure

Deep in a hollow tree
sits a baby squirrel
watching as a bird flies by
it's wings all a swirl

He peeks out of the hole
to see the world around
and climbs slowly from the tree
to explore the unknown ground

He sees the flowers and the sun
he finds an acorn near
he scurries up the tree to home
he hurries out of fear

Deep in the tree now he sleeps
his adventure at an end
maybe tomorrow he'll come out
or maybe he'll stay in

SUNBEAMS

The desert sun lay waiting
behind the golden mountain
it's beams of burning fire
burst forth like a fountain

They flew across the morning sky
with such amazing grace
and warmed the very hearts
of every hidden face

They kissed the sleeping heads
of every little flower
and turned the darkest moment
into the brightest hour

They crept across the shadowed land
and over the ocean fair
they melted the snowy mask
of winter that was there

They knocked upon my window
with a tender sound
when I tried to find them
they were nowhere around

I called to them out loud
to please come down and play
but it was time for them
to softly fly away.

TENNIS SHOES

Far back in the closet sits
a pair of old tennis shoes
They were white years ago,
but now have seen their better days
I cannot bring myself to throw
away these ragged, worn out shoes
For they were my very first
pair I wore when I was just brand new

THE POET-THE POEM

How does a poem come to be
it's very hard to say
the poet had a thought
that grew along the way

It passes thru the poet's heart
and fills his very being
it reaches deep inside
and leads the soul to seeing

The words don't come easy
it's very hard to write
the poet is the master
that brings it to light

With love and laughter
the poet helps it grow
with pen and paper
the words just seem to flow

The poet is an artist
with a canvas bare
the masterpiece he creates
is beyond compare.

The Rose Ellen Mary McGee Ordeal

Two little girls were sitting by a garden gate
One was seven and the other nearly eight
They were having a party of afternoon tea
With their dollies, Clara and Rose Ellen Mary McGee.
They were all dressed in their bonnets of blue
They had cakes and cookies and sandwiches, too
The little girls were laughing, having a good time
When there occurred such a terrible crime.

Out through the gate came a horrible beast
A big black, hairy dog looking for a feast
He ran to the table and began to eat
Both girls screamed and jumped to their feet.
The girl of eight grabbed for her dolly's arm
To keep Rose Ellen Mary McGee from harm
The beast turned out to be much faster
Now the doll was headed for sure disaster.

Around and around the tree they all went
Till all three were completely spent
They fell upon the ground by a bush of holly
The dog started panting and dropped the dolly.
Rose Ellen Mary McGee with hair full of dirt
Was wet and soggy, but not really hurt
The little girl hugged her dolly near
"I'm so very sorry." she said. "My dear."
"Please forgive me for not protecting you."
"I'm sorry you were frightened, too."
Forgiveness comes to all creatures that be
Dogs, girls of eight or Rose Ellen Mary McGee.

THOUGHTS

To late I see
what became of me
I lost myself somewhere
 along the way
do I search for tomorrow?
or drift back to yesterday?
here I sit aware of it
to love, to hate
a world create
I must try
I know not why
my dream, a scheme
of lessor deeds
return to me
in unsown seeds
where do I go?
I do not know
alone am I
to laugh, to cry
my story ends, like it begins
a smile, a tear again I fear
what is not there, I cannot share.

TIME

Time passes by
without rhyme or reason
slowly changing days
with the passing seasons

We are here
we are gone
always together
always alone

Time takes our lives
without caring
takes our dreams
with such daring

Are we free?
Are we sure?
Are we lost?
Are we pure?

Time passes by
within a single day
never knowing where
or which way

Make your time count
use every single minute
for we are only here
as a resident and tenant

TO MEND A HEART

Today I found a broken heart
that had fallen on the ground
it lay there so lonely
with no one else around

I reached down and picked it up
and with a tender word
I began to mend it
as a broken wing upon a bird

I took a golden thread of love
and sewed the hope back in
then I gave it caring
to start over again

Soon the heart filled with pride
and ready to start a new
I put it back where it belonged
I gave it back to you.

Today......

The fragrance of your hair
lingers in a faded shawl,
your bible is open wide
on the table down the hall.

In quiet wonder they pass by
to see you resting there,
in dress of blue cotton
and silver in your hair.

You are my inspiration
the reason why I sing,
the tears and the laughter
you are my everything.

You are resting Mother
and soon I'll see you there,
now I will let you go
for you are in God's care.

Treasure Hunt

Today I went on a treasure hunt
from the front yard to the back
the things I discovered there
would fill a gunny sack
underneath a blooming bush
I found a pair of pants
they were just lying there
upon a hill of ants
up in a big oak tree
I found a broken kite
my son tried to fly
in the middle of the night
back in the dark corner
of an old wooden shed
I found a lovely dolly
with a crooked head
in the back yard by the pool
I found a baseball hat
and when I picked it up
I found a baby rat
over by the picket fence
I saw a big red ball
I thought that I had finished
but that wasn't all
underneath the steps
I saw a shining face
it was my two year old
in his hiding place
pants, kites, hat, ball and dolly
are not treasures you say
they are to those who lost them
somewhere along the way
my treasure hunt is over now as
I turn to go inside there is not a
place left unturned for anything to hide

TURTLE

A turtles a strange sight to see
He doesn't look like you or me
He has no arms, he has no hair
He has eyes, but no eyebrows there
His body's made of hard round shell
He cannot talk, he cannot yell
The way he walks is very slow
How he runs I do not know
The wrinkled skin is old and worn
The shell is sometimes broke or torn
When troubles near he goes inside
What a perfect place to hide
He may not care about a hurdle
After all he's just a turtle
He never has a care at all
Unless he takes a nasty fall
He walks all day to go a mile
He has no laugh, he has no smile
Is there a stranger thing to see
Ask a turtle, don't ask me !!!!!

UPON A SHELF

Pictures upon a dusty shelf
living there all by themselves
worn out smile, faded eyes
finds the spot where memories lie

Little children now are grown
with a family of their own
taking pictures that will last
on a dusty shelf from the past.

WAITING MEMORIES

Upon the shelves of time
are memories end to end
of all the good and bad we know
all the long lost friends

We take them down now and then
to dust the dirt away
and replace them back again
to recall another day

Memories are forever
so the saying goes
we will never lose them
as the feelings grow

So upon the shelf they sit
waiting for a chance to fall
when we start to remember
each and every one and all

WHAT CAN THE MATTER BE

Sitting on the sidewalk
all forlorn and blue
a tattered child of four
looking for a clue

Freckled face smiling
eyes of blue a glow
golden hair upon his head
a small face full of woe

Tattered pants with patches
holey shoes and ragged shirt
a small and lovely child
who is so full of hurt

Did he lose his wagon?
did he forget his way?
did someone hurt him?
what has he to say?

Has someone left him?
has he lost his dog?
such a simple reason
seems he lost his frog!

WHAT I THOUGHT I SAW

As I sat among the trees
and splendored at their awe
you will never, ever believe
what I thought I saw

There was a family of blackbirds
walking through the grass
one turned to the other and said
now we've got class

There was a father bird
in a denim suit
the mother wore a gingham dress
which was so very cute

They were pushing a baby carriage
with two baby birds inside
as they passed beside me
both the children cried

They seemed to be headed somewhere
I'm sure they'll be there soon
and as the sunlight faded
they vanished with the moon

WHAT IS A SON

He's a walking book of questions........a never-ending source of energy......full of mischief.....full of love....a discoverer....yet an explorer....even though he's tough....he still needs a hug and kiss when he gets a boo-boo.......He laughs....he cries....pesters the babysitter.....jumps in mud puddles in his new shoes.....he pulls the cat's tail....watches cartoons with his brothers.......falls asleep in his mother's arms.......doesn't eat spinach......but sneaks cookies.....he's dads fishing buddy......a bundle of joy.....a wonder to his family.....mama's little man......God's precious angel.....the reason that makes life worth living.

WHAT IS.......
(the color of silence)

The secrets I keep are
Hidden bruises and broken bones
Eyes covered concealing scars

Constant anger and abuse
Others will never see
Letting myself have hope
Often wanting death to come
Revealing truth to no one

Only one thing left to do
Finally I see the way

Silently waiting in fear
I am ready now
Listening for footsteps
Every heartbeat echoes
Nearer, nearer he comes
Can't stop, red flows forth
Everything over, freedom comes.

WHERE

Where are the flowers?
that grew by the wall
they were once roses
blooming in the Fall

Where are the butterflies?
with gossamer wings
multi-colored canvas
that came in the Spring

Where are the song birds?
whose melody would enter
all the frozen hearts
through the coldest Winter

Where are the rabbits?
wake from their slumber
that bring about
the lazy days of Summer

Whiskers

A cat has whiskers
Why are they there
Are they part of his face
Or part of his hair
Above his eyes around his nose
They seem to fool with
 him where ever he goes
Do they help him to catch
 mice or maybe to smell
I ask my cat but he wouldn't tell
They are long and silky
 and mostly white
Do they help him see in
 the dark of night
What good are they I have no clue
Have they been there forever
Or are they brand new
My cats not talking
He'll say not a word
When I ask him he thinks I'm absurd
I know not the reason
Why whiskers are there
and to tell the truth
I simply don't care.

WINTER ENVY

I live in the California desert
each day is sunny and bright
in the middle of winter
that doesn't seem so right
There is no snow or bitter cold
not much chance of it, I'm told
Sisters in Missouri, it's ten below
has five inches of ice and six foot of snow

She can make snowmen and snow ice cream
frozen streets and frozen streams
she can go sledding in the bitter wind
drink hot cocoa with a friend
Cuddle up close, bundle up tight
go ice skating in the moonlight
sit by the fire all rosy and red
wear hats and earmuffs on her head

Mittens on her hands for extra heat
oh, my that does sound so sweet
bitter cold, ice, and ten below
frozen streams covered with snow
I ask her to send snowballs by mail
but all attempts seem to fail
she froze them and sent them rush
when I got them, they were mush

No cutting wood at six below
no wading through ten foot snow
no freezing nights and icy days
winter envy leads me astray
I have my desert each day I wake
and starry night without flakes
I'm thankful for the sun's warm light
If I were there I'd have frostbite

WITHOUT

A poem without rhyme
has to have a reason
as a year without time
may end with the season

A sky without clouds
is as clear as a bell
a life without heaven
is surely a hell

A world without love
is a sad lonely place
a man without life
is a nameless face

A nation without peace
is a place for war
as the people die
it will be no more

A mind without thought
is a wasted thought
a voice without song
nevermore will sing

A poem without end
goes on forever
it makes a poet
a man who is clever

YARD SALE ?

Quite a laughing sight to see,
yard sale shopping, mom, sis and me
unlike anything you've ever seen,
without a doubt we are the queens
every Saturday morning out the door by eight,
got to hurry can't be late
eyes wide open for signs on poles,
nailed on trees, letters so bold

Nothing or no one gets in our way,
we mean business on yard sale day
off to the right a sign appears,
mom yells stop, right now, right here
first one out she heads for the gate,
opens a box and finds a plate
yellow sale sign by the U-Haul on the street,
it's a moving sale, how neat

across the yard I spot a chair,
a 4 drawer dresser and a bear
roses of blue on a table in a vase,
sis has a doll with a clown face
dresses of every color and shape,
mom is ready with measuring tape
shoes and purses box upon box,
gloves and belts, slips and socks

Antique jewelry, American flag,
seems kind of strange there are no tags
lipsticks. perfumes, hats of red,
scarfs and bonnets to fit my head
everything gathered we get ready to go,
mom stops and yells, oh no!
she drops her bags at her feet,
this is not the sale, it's across the street !!!!

YOUR CHILD

I am your child
mother of six
why did you sell me?
for a fix

I am your child
father in the crowd
why did you do?
what was not allowed

I am your child
American born
hungry and crying
tattered and worn

I am your child
let freedom ring
take me home
where angels sing

Z-Z-Z-Z-Z-Z-Z (SNORING)

I've been told I snore
but how can this be
I stayed awake one night
so I could listen to me

I only heard silence
not a sound ensued
I woke my husband
so he could hear too

About daylight I began
to doze
there in the darkness
a faint sound arose

It started so gently
this sudden refrain
then all of a sudden
I heard a freight train

It passed through the bedroom
over the floor
and as I awoke
it went out the door

My husband was still,
sleeping peacefully
the sound I heard
came from him, not me

Like a miller who saws
wood in the daylight
my husband drives trains
through our house at night.

www.ingramcontent.com/pod-product-compliance
Lightning Source LLC
Chambersburg PA
CBHW031204160426
43193CB00008B/493